1

Journey of a Hypnosis practitioner against cancer

Christophe Pank

Table des matières

Author of :

1/ My first steps on the Law of Attraction (Feb 2013)

2/ Hypnosis and Pain Management : The study of the Hypno-Analgesia Process (Jul 2015)

3/ Limited Power : Accepting our own limits is to open up our real potential (May 2016)

4/ Hyperempiria and Self-Mastery : Apply Hyperempiria for your personal development (Jul 2017)

Introduction

When you say the word cancer, there is a particular **fear** which appears on the face of our interlocutors.

Indeed, this illness seems to be **anchored** in the collective unconscious. And many of our close ones share a memory or have strong feelings about it. This booklet's goal is to present my perception as a **therapist when we are living through this sickness**. The ambition of these few words is not to answer the issue of cancer. I would like to just share my story, simply, with the **different reflections and realisations** I had during this time.
Today, it has been a little more than **two years** that I do not have any tumor, I am not just yet considered as 'healed' according to the medical staff, the delay being five years to validate a healing, however, it doesn't influence the words I am about to share with you.

I will share the **different experiences** I put in place in order to **handle cancer**, different reflections I had on the subject and the results obtained.

Chapter 1 : At the beginning…

I had the chance to practice well being processes since I discovered **martial arts** when I was a teenager.

I discovered **Ki/Chi (internal energy in oriental traditions)** when I was only seeing martial arts as combat practice. Then, by studying and encountering many teachers, I discovered that the ancient combat masters were often **healing practitioners.** This made me realise that our natural capacity permits us to **appease with touch.** I was able to put in practice the **energetic touch** on many wounds. I can't be sure that the Ki wasn't the reason of the positive results I had, but it had a strong impact on me. It is also possible that the **auto-suggestion,** as described **by Emile Coué,** played a role in these phenomenoms, however, from this moment, I plunged myself into these processes.

With time, and higher education, I learnt about the **NLP.** It is an excellent process to **communicate better with yourself and others.** This tool offers excellent techniques **to reach your goals. And practice will be crucial** in this apprenticeship. In the energetic world or in the subconscious one, I practiced everything I learned. No encounter is insignificant and my path made me meet many people, the ones who were able to help me in my development and apprenticeship.

With years, and naturally, I was able to receive my first partners. I saw that these techniques were **bringing peace and well being**.

On the other hand, the more you discover, **the more you have questions**…more and more complex. For some of them, there are is no answer. I often asked myself **how I would handle a serious illness** if I was to have one. This imposes sincerity on ourself and how we view death.

It is a question that many of us wonder about. And we don't obtain answers necessarily. As a practitioner, it is possible that your role will bring you to consider this question under a new light. **Would my process be able to help me as it helps my partners ?** In my perception of the world, a heavy illness **should not be treated by modern medicine**, it is more a secondary path (Do not get me wrong, I invite all sick people to **consult a doctor** as soon as he/she has symptoms). Maybe, it comes from **too big of an ego** and a belief too **deterministic**. The thing is that I believe that we were born to live for a period of time and that we are going to die when we should die. Nature **offers us a potential** and if we didn't have all this new technology, maybe we would have died already. So, with this **thinking, quite limiting**, my point of view was that either a **sickness will take me away**, or I **would find a solution** through energetic care, massages, naturopathy or other psychological approaches.

The truth, is that we do not know what will be our reaction **until we are confronted** with the situation. All of the rest is only speculation. It is very easy to **say many things** to many people around us, or, to ourselves, when **the situation is only a possible scenario of life**. What do we do when the situation is no longer a possibility…but a fact ? I remember when I was reading Robbins, a NLP coach, explaining that we can through our **internal dialogue, change things.** Or, another time, when I was reading about tai-chi principles in which the body energy offers a path to a better being. I was questioning a lot on **how do we apply concretely these processes**. A movie that had an impact on me a lot, with Jim Carrey, is 'Man on the Moon'. In this movie, the character who lived a lot got sick with cancer. He looks for a while to get out of it and starts many different spiritual quests and using different tools more or less mystical. At the end, he dies. This character, being a bit eccentric and very manipulative towards others for the sake of the show, reflects on the fact that **all of this world is only an illusion**. This **kind** of movie was prompting me to know if I am not only in a **belief, an illusion**…

To strech it, I was wondering if **I was not a con artist**. Who, and even if the results on my partners were impressing, wasn't only proposing **suggestion of possibilities.**

When ideas become reality, when life offers you a new experience, then, **there are no more doubts** to have, there are no more questions without answers…there is only one thing to do, **to get on with it and to do your best**.
I put myself in a sickness, which would allow me to **experiment** and verify the veracity of my convictions. Did you ever wonder, **if, we were not building our own sicknesses ?** I do, and knowing my personnality, I think I **put in place this experience in my life**.

I use the semantic '**experience**' because it is what I used when I was talking about my illness. An experience is **completely neutral**, there is only the result which is positive or negative. I was able **to put in practice what I knew,** as an **initiatory phase**. It is like the **martial art approach**, going from the technique to the fight as soon as possible. An approach of the truth, which is **as much in the therapy as the fight**, represents the pathway I feel comfortable in and like. For those who follow me, you know I **always question everything** and that my starting point is that nothing is true except what I can see, live and feel. This is quite empirical…

Chapter 2 : The discovery

We are in November 2008.

Following a training session, during which I took a kick in my private parts, looking to see if nothing was hurt, I realised that I had a small ball on one of my testicles. At first, I thought **it was a bruise.** I didn't worry that much. For those who know about **Enneagram types,** my profile is eight. It is a type of personality of someone who is strongly **in denial.** To maintain **the illusion to be strong**, the eight profile types develop the capacity to **not feel, see, hear** hurtful things. I often explain that denial can be good. However, with time, **denial makes the good become execrable.** I am not going to pay any attention to this ball **which decided to lodge in me.** Sometimes, I was working with energy on it, **but without real conviction.** I thought it was weird…but didn't go further in my thoughts.

I wasn't really digging… unconsciously, I didn't want to know. I prefer to take care of it, myself, when it will bother me… You need to understand with this idea of being 'strong', I don't want to be helped, so I almost never bother to go to the doctor. I always **think** that I can manage alone. For example, when I learn a new method, everything I can have goes through the filter of the technique. It was the case after a training in **aromatherapy**, I experimented with for months…

Then, as **I never believe what is written** without validating it, I let you imagine the big mistakes and the very negative feedbacks I received... Because I always prefer to find my answers, I work **with what I know or I will study what I do not know** yet and that will make me better.

This case was no exception...

Chapter 3 : Then, trouble started

While I was denying this issue, which wasn't a nuisance just yet, I continued to **train myself and to receive** my partners.

I worked on **serious illnesses** and have been entrusted to accompany some of my partners **until their last breath.** It gave me **a certain distance** regarding my profession. I realised that **I couldn't save or help everyone** and sometimes, it is hard to accept. As many practitioners, I was suffering **the complex of the saviour.** I wish I could save the whole world. I remember, in some meditations where it happened I was suggesting to myself things like 'I wish some people suffered less, even if I have to take on some of their pain'. It is what we call a **compulsion** in the Enneagram type. **To believe that you are strong enough** to take on somebody's else suffering but to finally realise that it is **extremely egotistic.** It took me years to lose myself less in this syndrome. Let's be sincere, I think that the saviour within me is still **a little too present today.**

Everything really started to speed up at a course about the **Silva Method.** I started to think that this little ball, still there, might deserve a little more of my attention.

Happy to be able to use this extraordinary method, I started to work on this ball through trance in **subjective communication.** Here is what came out of this trance.

No need to be a biological decoding bigshot to understand that at this level for men, there is a connection with sexuality, paternity, etc… The process is very easy, through a trance, I will connect myself with the sick part and start a **co-developed interaction** between conscious and subconscious. I quickly arrived on the heart of my problem, regarding children, the link to the father and my own capacity to become myself a father. This **paternity issue** is recurrent since childhood. I remember around 12 years of age, I was sleeping over at a friend's place, and we spent the evening, like many children, to think of the future. Without knowing it, we were using the hypnotic technique **'to pretend'** : act as if we were adults. One thing I remember, is that he wanted a house with a wife and children. My future was represented by one thing : **I was picturing myself, leaning over, with a skull on the desk and a candle to light up.** I remember saying that **I didn't want any children.** I also remember saying that I will **die alone**. At this point of the book, you probably think that I was **a bit strange** as a boy. And it is true, when I think of it, it makes me smile. This reflection **to not want children** comes from way back. My mother was, a few month ago, remembering me at 18 years of age, I told her not to wait for grandchildren on my side. With a little knowledge in psychology, we can easily see that we **smell a rat**.

 For years, I fought to **defend my opinion** in all conversations about children. With the eternal rhetorical answer that with time, I will change my mind.

Around 20 years old, I was able to put myself **in a rage** when imposed on me was the idea or possibility to have a child.

To come back to this **key session,** I realise the strong link with these different elements : me, to be a father, my relationship with fatherhood. This trance offered me to **straighten out this issue** and an obligation to **remove the denial** in place for so many years. The only symptom of this internal complexity, at this point, was yet just this little ball…all quiet. However, what I just **opened in me**, was about to have complex consequences… I believe that **we do not live what we are not able to**. That no pain comes our way if we can't overcome it. I often asked myself if to have this cancer, even if it is not a very dangerous cancer, wasn't an **alarm signal** which had to happen at this point within my life where **I was ready to work on it.**

Two days later, this little ball of no more than 0,2 cm became as big as half of my testical. And in a month, this ball became a tumor of approximately 280 grammes.

Chapter 4 : A few difficult months

In a few weeks only, I found myself with a **big problem**.

From the beginning of december 2011, it started to be a bit painful. And it is around Christmas that I had my first **big physical reaction to the tumor**.
I was at my mom's, evening time, on our way to eat with my father and my brother, I started to feel a heavy fatigue and a high temperature. Then, I found it hard to digest and the tumor, which was consolidating, was tiring me out. I know that at this time, I was **still in denial**. I am, now, using the word **tumor**, but back then, I was thinking that I had some **infection.** Then, a friend had a problem with one of his testicles aswell and he explained to me that there was a very common issue named **inguinal hernia.** Thinking of a **synchronicity** and being fully in **the unconscious will to know**, telling myself that a hernia could be an issue, was absolutely perfect.
However, after my winter return, I had the great opportunity to do a private lesson of Jiu Jitsu the 2nd January 2012. When I got up that morning, I was extremely feverish and the area where the tumor developed was extremely painful as too were my lower abdomen and liver.

Saying that, this session has been absolutely **horrible**, and I told myself that it would be very complicated to train and to be able to continue for the next few months. At this time, I was also putting in place training programmes and I wanted to write my first book. I gave myself until july to finish these projects.

Being at a milestone, I couldn't stop working. As many self-employed, **if we do not work, we do not live.** I started then **thorough research**, knowing that several symptoms were indeed recurrent. The pain in the tumor's area, liver pain, lower back pain, very high temperatures, and generally, a tiredness more and more heavy. It is around the 15th of January that in a **conscious awakening**, I started to look on the Internet to find all that it could be. The word **cancer** was coming back regularly. All my symptoms were similar and after a few days of **muscular testing signaling works, and many internal dialogues,** I came to the conclusion that it would be a cancer. Of course, I wasn't sure of it and I will receive confirmation of it…seven months later. When I say to my learners or partners who practice self-hypnosis or hetero hypnosis, that **subconscious can lie**, this step was a big fat lie for me. At first, **my conscious didn't want at all to admit** the idea of cancer. I remember that every night around this period, I worked on trances in which I was suggesting that the morning after, the testical was going to go back to **its normal state**.

It is **the principle of the magic thought**…really common in the energetic trend…it is indeed one of the defaults of these processes which persuades us that, in an instant, 'everything'can be solved.

You can easily imagine that **it didn't happen** and because suggestions were not having any **realistic intention**. Remember, goals need to be realist. When we question, it is important to **be ready to listen to the answer**, however, it is rarely the case. We can listen through **muscular testing, signaling, or even internal dialogue.** If we keep questioning, after the use of all these tools, it is because we know that **the answer is wrong.** We just want so much to have **an answer which would fit with what we are ready to hear** that **a doubt** would be the proof we are lying to ourselves. Before admitting the word 'cancer', I must **have tested myself hundreds of times**.

At the instant I admitted that potentially it was not a hernia but a cancer, I felt **appeased**. I am not saying I was feeling good, simply that the **constant dialogue** I was having about this issue started to become a **little bit more fluid**. I think it is only the last week of january that I really started to work a lot on myself. When I say a lot, it was even **excessive**. I was getting up early, I was going to bed late and often my nights were more looking like **trances** than sleep.

Chapter 5 : Work on myself

The first step was very simple

Early, each morning, I put in place **auto-hypnosis sessions in auto-suggestions**. Knowing the positive results of the **subjective communication** offered in less than 48h, a beautiful huge tumor…I decided to focus on this process. I will come back to it later. It is interesting to see that often, the work we have done on ourself before and for years, via meditation, energetic processes or auto-hypnosis, **limits us**. **This limit is not on purpose**, but we do not necessarly want to touch the deeper level of ourselves. It is like a **protection from the conscious** of the subconscious to avoid living a **pain** or even more, **to put into question our life**.

When we say to ourselves that the illness within us can **really hurt you (everything is relative)**, even kill us, we have to make **a detour from the critical factor**, a link between the conscious and the subconscious. I was able to find an answer to my question…how would I react if I was to become ill. The answer, just to constantly work on one goal… You know that in the definition of our goals, there is an important aspect : **focusing**. When we are sick, most of the external elements **take a different place**. We have then the opportunity **to focus on what is essential**. Our body, one way or another, will remind us that we are in pain, in discomfort or with other psychic issues.

To focus, this is **an excellent element**. I think it is probably one of things that is put in place **the most naturally** and that will help the psychic of a human being. Indeed, all this discomfort, created by the sickness, **orientates constantly our conscious and subconscious towards this hurt**. We can decide to **ignore** it, sometimes even some people hate this constant feeling of being sick. However, if we succeed to orientate our **natural focusing,** that we put in place on our discomfort, like a goal and that it is well orientated…it becomes a **powerful lever** to reach your goal. In my case, it has been an **excellent stimulant** to really **spend time to work on myself and observe the effetcs that it could have.** My objective was simple, it was to **remove completely the tumor.** Of course, I didn't know at all if that was possible, the only case I heard of on that matter were stories I read about in some books. For that matter, it is a question I wondered about as I never met someone who succeeded to remove a heavy sickness, I had the feeling that it was more **positive stories, motivating, than real facts and reality.**

A few years ago, I participated in this course about a process called **mirror body.** Brofmann is the creator of this method and also an elder of the Silva method. He put in place his own method following an illness, a brain cancer. It was said that with the work of Silva, meditations, visualisations, etc… **he was able to heal himself**.

Having participated in his course and experienced this for a decade, I observed **really interesting things** and very **positive** feedback. It can seem a bit odd, for some of you, that I told myself that it was **a good thing that I was able to live an illness like this**. For me, it was like a **challenge** and most of all a **path towards the truth**. The one I was proposing to my partners and the one which for me was **just in my daily life.** All of this period, even if there had been a lot of hurt and some important issues, offered me the possibility to **really deepen my processes.**

Whether in auto-hypnosis or in energetic, I used everything I studied and practice for years. I lived **in the factual**, it allowed me to put aside techniques which were **intellectually interesting and stimulating** but really efficient in my case. Every morning, I put in place a work of **auto-hypnosis and energetic.** If you have done courses in energetic, you can see that trances are part of this process. If we look at the history of hypnosis, **Mesmerism**, at the origin of the modern discipline, was linking **trances and the psychomagnetic.** I have worked on **somnanbulant trance** in internal dialogue. It allowed me to settle in the first place the different subjects which were putting me in **dissonant emotions**. In my emotions spectrum, the most present was **anger**. It permitted me to validate many regressions and other perceptions. Regularly, I put forward that the subconscious wants to **express itself**.

It is during this period that I realised that auto-hypnosis, only in **direct suggestions, were quite limited**. It is important to have a **correct semantic.** However, even with this notion, with a cancer, it is not enough. To be more precise, if you have an illness a bit heavy, a suggestion like '**I am doing better and better,**' may look like a **refusal to listen to your own illness**. I am not saying that you can't work with suggestions. Only that it is important to **include this tool** as part of the work that we put in place. Moreover, it is interesting to understand that with my psyche, I need to work on different elements. **Subconscious and Unconscious.** Subconscious picks up emotions, values and beliefs, recurrent schemes. Unconscious works on **symptoms** of the body. At that moment, the only way for me to work on unconscious was to apply **trances in ultra.** I will come back to this later.

Once I was able to observe that direct suggestions should be more, as advised it Joseph Murphy, a **continued repetition** in my daily life, I focused principally on auto-analysis through q&a, sometimes conscious, sometimes unconscisous. Feedbacks were physiological, the tumor **was changing size** and more or less painful. It also offered **symbolic regressions** and sometimes even **past lives**. I believe that regressions in past life are only solutions that we find through our subconscious to **facilitate a change.**

All actions I was puttiong into place in my daily life, while cleaning my apartment, riding my motorcycle, going to train, eating…had a goal, '**make the tumor disappear**'.

For example, on my motorcycle, I had for 7 months the same **visualisation work** each time that I rode it. The principle was easy : To take the tumor as the weight of some things in my life. As it is difficult to make a good questionning, I proposed the suggestion that it was everything representing what I cumulated without even being conscient of it. I always have a backpack with me, I was imagining that **this bag was full of my hurts**, and that as soon as I was riding, I was discharging it on the road…always behind myself. This tool permitted me to calm down some pains and to continually work on the idea to **let go of things**, to not keep them in me. In my opinion when we are sick, **everything is a possible exercise** towards a better being. It is a **necessary discipline.** I will come back on the importance of sport in my practice, I only give you an idea now of what was important in this personal dynamic, in the process put in place. A friend, with whom I was sharing a lot of reflections on therapy, has the same vision of care and partners as myself. He often puts forward **that psyche needs to be worked on as much as the body.** It is true that most of the time, when we work with a method, we put aside all the other tools. However, we are complex beings : **physical, psychic and energetic.** When I was training, the goal was to keep the sickness in guard. This symbolic, taken from martial arts, of the **practitioner forging his/her blade to cut off his/her ego,** would definitely fit my approach.

I now wonder why I didn't go to see a doctor, when the discomfort was so strong and daily. The answer is simple and full of ego, **I didn't want anybody's help.** I somehow always have the feeling that when something happens, I need **first to find my answers and do my best.** Even if it gets worse. It is purely a **compulsion** of my personality. Indeed, there is in me and for me, this desire to **not appear weak**. I can say that in my daily life, it is not the thing which brings me the most benefits. It is like a child who would have hurt himself and doesn't want to be taken care of because he wants to act as grown up.

The word 'cancer' was not yet said to me, so I was also able to stay in a form of **denial.** The direct benefit of this way to operate, is that I was sure that I was able to **go over** what I was living. I was rarely staying at home when I was a child, my parents were saying it was ok. I admit that it was positive, only it doesn't really make one open him/herself **to listen to him/herself.** It is actually a subject to ponder. Do we have to constantly lose ourselves in the sickness signs, even if that means being obsessional, or just to let things getting better ? I do not have any answers, even if I think that we should **learn to develop a fair listening** to our body and spirit. Unfortunately, it is not culturally taught, at least in our western culture.
With this way to think, I almost didn't talk at all of what was happening. I have tendancy to **keep things for me and to not communicate** in these moments. Many people were upset I didn't share with them afterwards.

In my opinion, there is no interest in making our loved ones panic or stress. It is better to go all the way and manage ourselves by dimishing the pressure everyone would have. I will come back to this because it is impressive to observe how much sickness can **distress** others.

To resume basic works :

1 – Internal dialogue and energetic each morning and evening.
2 – While riding my motorcycle, symbolic work on the backpack.
3 – While training, projection of a fight with myself.
It was about **four or five hours** of daily work.

Chapter 6 : Pain management

From January to mid-July 2012, the tumor was settled.

It was heavy and so very painful in my daily life. As I was saying previously, there were **pains from the tumor** itself, but also an **acute sensation from my lower abdomen,** as my liver was pulled and compressed. More and more I had a huge pain in my **lower back** and this was giving me quite sleepless nights.

Hypnosis is an excellent **analgesic tool, even anesthetic.** It is besides, a method which starts to be reinstated in hospitals for some surgery. I was able to test a lot on **pain management.** The latter was taking different forms. It allowed me to create **anchors, key suggestions** but also **deep trances.** I was also able to observe if **analysis work,** awareness were offering appeasement aswell. In a day, I was having a **continued pain of 4** on a scale of 1 to 10. In a few minutes, it was also possible to climb to 7 and so becoming very uncomfortable. I was usually meeting with some self-employed friends to talk about different projects and exchange over many subjects. Every Wednesday. Each time, after an hour of discussion, pain was coming to disturb me. It took a while before I was able to find a technique to calm this pain. It is with a spatial anchor that I succeed. I was **focusing on a logo** from a shop at the beginning of the discussion, to anchor it at a moment where I was fine, and as soon as the pain was coming back,

I was focusing back on the logo. It was very common that the pain became so strong that I was being **delirious or that I was vomitting.** It is with these observations that I understood the limits of auto-hypnosis on pain. It is **impossible to handle your pain when the temperature of your body becomes too high.** In general, pain could have been reoriented or diminished by going down in **somnabulant trances.** With suggestions and enough relaxation, the pain could pass. With a temperature, we are at a completely **instable** somnanbulant level. We are easily going to be **hallucinating** and our thoughts are going in all directions, just as it would be in **paradoxical sleep.** When my nights were too painful, I worked in **deep trances**. The issue is that I wasn't mastering my timings. **Time distorsion** made a few hours seem like a few minutes. The big strength of H-Ultras is to permit a **well being state at 0 level of pain.** I wanted to work more when I was in Esdaile, the problem is that the well being was completely drugging me and **only allowed me to recuperate**.

As I was saying previously, I worked a lot with **internal dialogues.** These longer sessions were permitting a **symbolic work,** which was offering interesting variations of perceptions. One of my first assumptions was that the sickness, and moreover the pain, were tools which give us **an indication.** This indication being that there is a **dissonant element,** or at least, that we need to pay attention to a few elements which **doesn't offer an internal harmony.**

In other words, if the pain grows stronger, it is probably because **I am going away** from what I need to deal with. If it is appeased, It is because I am getting closer and that **I am treating** the issue. When I was going into this **subjective dialogue**, I was finding **ways to flee.** For example by **sleeping or confusing myself,** meaning that I couldn't handle my thoughts. These sessions, I was to consider them empty. Other times, the cursor of pain was changing many times, especially on some questions touching some emotions, pains. **Transitional pain** is a way we have to live out a trauma or a resistance. It is the reason why sessions were sometimes very long. It allowed me to see important points, separate them from the less important points and step by step walk towards the sources to both **physical and emotional pain**. The questioning and the awareness was often generating a huge pain from the resistance of an inside scheme I was shaking and a **physical appeasement replaced by a psychic discomfort**. Better to say that sometimes, the pain of the body is **easier** to handle than the spirit which loses itself in downturns and perceptions. Some regressions also had the **capacity to appease physical pain**. I had the feeling that this sickness was cumulating many hurts from my childhood which crystallised, only to reappear here and there. To finish, the energetic linked to a trance, opened new possibilities as well which were very interesting. The touch became an **awareness of my body** and of its capacity to appease itself.

These last methods worked at different times. There were indeed many parameters to take into consideration. It only takes to be in an emotional state for **some tools to become inoperative.**

I believe that there is **always a way to dimisish and handle your pain**. The only thing we need to **manage is our temperature**. The only solution I found, as I don't take any medication, **was cold baths and showers.**

Even if at the time, it wasn't agreeable, it offers us the possibility to take back the control of our dashboard.

Chapter 7 : Martial arts

I think therefore I am, I fight therefore I am.

Writing these words make me smile at my **compulsion** as defined in the Enneagram, in this belief that **the world is a fight.** Facts being what they are, **I am a fighter** and have been since my adolescence. I like it, it is a time where 'I am'. During all my work on myself, **I never stopped training.** I firmly believed in Budo (Japonese martial arts) since a child. I do not practice it to be strong, but to become a man who can **overcome all trials** and reinforce my 'blade', this challenge to the ego. When I went to do my first course of the year and that I suffered, **I wasn't proud.** I realised for the first time that in addition to the symptoms I lived with, it was also impacting my body in a really problematic way. When I saw my grand father die, I thought to myself that he was dead because he stopped going out, to move. The **metaphor of the tree** is interesting. A sprout is **supple, moves a lot,** sometimes is tossed around, but **full of life.** Dying trees become rigid, branches are breaking in the wind. I concluded that inaction, the fade of the body from memory while aging and maybe sick, was leading to death. Strange enough, even if I can't say that trainings were easy, often during the course, **symptoms and pains were diminishing, even disappearing.** It is curious that sickness and sport are taboo. There is some kind of **awkwardness** about this subject. And when we think about it, it is true that at the beginning of the year, we ask for an **aptitude certificate** specially made for sport and given by a doctor.

Yet sport, which is an **excellent palliative** to depression, pains and discomforts is often forbidden to the ones who suffer from some illnesses. We can prevent a positive thing and with good intention : **to protect the patient...**

I am convinced that if **we would open the consciousness** of sick people, even if sometimes it may be difficult, or even painful, we would find real complementary alternatives (only prerequisite : to like sport), benefits would be real. This year, I went into competition. For me, **training became therapy**. When I started Karate, I had an important blood deficiency, I was lacking 70% of iron. **Trainings were hell.** I was scared, I was hurt, I was coming back home and I was vomitting... A form of masochism, of **sublimation, very martial,** of the pain being an instructor of the man I was becoming. Let's be sincere, **it was horrible.** I think that as a practitioner, these beginnings have been **the most difficult**. On the other hand, it has been a learning curve which was useful against my cancer. **I can overcome much more than what I think I can**. I remember of one of my Senseis who told me that when I am tired, when I just can't anymore, when I vomit violenlty, **I still have 40% of my energy,** and so that I need to not think that I am at the end of myself. I think that this philosophy **helped me a lot** in my daily life. The counterpart of this is that I can be quite harsh with people who complain...I probably didn't understand quite yet the subtleties of this teaching...When I was entering my dojo, I **wasn't fighting my partners,** when I was going for competition, I wasn't winning by being on the podium...simply to be able to go, to dare, to share a moment in this world that I love so much, was already a **daily victory.**

Symbolically, I imagined that every fight, every technique I did, was **strengthening me, healing me.**

As I said previously, everything that we do when we are sick has a **unique goal to heal.** The symbolic of the cells fighting really is a physical fight, understanding strengths and weaknesses. I am lucky to practice **Luta Livre and Jiujitsu.** The philosophy of these supple arts is extraordinary. It teaches to **not oppose yourself to force,** but to perceive it differently, to orientate it and to orientate yourself differently. When a technique doesn't work, you just need to find another one and to **apply the right angle,** exactly like in therapy. When we are sick, there are multiple methods, **everyone looks for his/her Holy Grail.** However, like in fights, we are all different against sickness. We do not react to the same thing, we do not accept the same values and beliefs. We then must find what brings us a **maximum of efficiency and a minimum of effort (JiuJitsu Principle).** Our body and our spirit might be weakened by the sickness, environement, doctors, medicine, **negative internal dialogues.** I think that to become a **Jiujitsu fighter against your sickness**, it is to learn to understand its strength, its place, its messages aswell. It is **to find the angles,** levers which will change your way to go about it, to fight. There will always be moments where **pressure** of the opponent (sickness) **will push us to give up.** However, we learn to **slow down its progression,** to handle it, to destabilize it and to defeat it. Masters I had, always told me, when you are in the 's....', **go back to your posture. Posture being your base.** Sometimes, it is hard to balance the fight as we are alone against the opponent, no coach in the corner who will **give us advice.** I did the majority of my fight without coaches, I was alone to handle things, and I think that **what we are on a tatami represents what we are in life.** Competitions I made in this time were pretty **painful.** I am used to fight, the stress, even if still present, is not what freezes me.

Fights I was in at this time were delicate. Outside of the pain, which in this ambiance doesn't help to pacify your being, **temperature** appearing unannounced. I felt **a huge peace** during the after fights, as if I overcame the belief that because we are 'sick, we can't perform anymore.

Without martial arts, which are by nature an anchor in a **very positive trance,** I wouldn't have lived this period of time the same. So, an advice, even if you are unwell, continue what stimulates you, it is a form of **fight between two trances,** two states, the one where you are sick and the one where you are fine.

Chapter 8 : H-Ultras Trances or Deep Trances

In my approach, I used a lot **deep trances**.

I never had worked yet on a **Sichort state,** but I did have the chance to study, to see **Esdaile**. For those who do not know hypnosis, it is what we call a **Hypnotic Coma. The Hypnotic Coma has nothing to do with the clinical coma.** As in hypnosis, we do not sleep, Esdaile defines a level of depth of trance. Just a note, the word 'Coma' comes from **Dave Elman**, the trend I developed my perception of hypnosis (another school from the one of **Milton Erickson**). What is interesting are effects of the deep trances. The first thing is the **appeasing state.** At this level, we are in a well being and happiness bubble. To be more precise, in **Hypnosophy, this semantic** means a trance particularly **subconscious.** The second thing is **analgesis, even a complete anesthesia.** When we are in a continued state of pain for days, with high and low variations, it is a pleasure to not feel your body. I used a lot this trance, sometimes excessively, I stayed in this level **for hours**…2-3 sometimes 4 hours. At this period of time, there were plenty of books by James Esdaile, especially since 1950, in the USA, which were indicating that these **deep levels were affecting the body,** and opened possibilities of quick healing.

Ramey, a specialist of the Ultra Depth, sells his method as a tool allowing, at these deep levels, to **accelerate healing...**My question : how do we know **if we are indeed in a quick healing** ? Is there a rhythm and a time to heal ?

Anyway, this level offers a **concrete path** to allow your being to not 'feel'sick, for a few minutes or hours. Just like a deep sleep which permits you to feel good. When I wasn't succeeding to go in this trance, because of the temperature, physical or psychic discomforts, I was certainly (I know that now) **between the somnanbulant level and the Esdaile level.** In this state, I wasn't resting but more in a **work of hypnosophy** (a form of hypno-analysis) very powerful. So much that sometimes during my sessions **my pains were exploding**, I was going into **spontaneous symbolic regressions**, which were so violent, because associated, that I was vomitting.

Returns into conscious were on the opposite **more peaceful,** in general, I was emotionally so empty, that my body and my spirit just wanted to sleep.

Chapter 9 : Simonton's Method

The first time I heard of Simonton, it was by one of my mentors, **Madame Lee Pascoe,** who was speaking about it during a **Silva method speech.**

It is a method based on Alpha works, a form of **auto-hypnosis.** Simonton is an **american oncologist and a radiotherapist** who put forward the importance and the possibilities that allows psychological treatment during cancer. He made a study of 71-78 which showed that survival was **twice as long** on terminal phases. As in the whole book, **I am not saying that this is a truth,** I just found the idea interesting and so I bought his two books, worked on his concepts. Nothing revolutionary but **a lot of discipline and visualisation.** Take an image of your cells in good health which **fight the sick ones.** During **long periods,** put in place this visualisation. What is great with the Internet and everything that we see on TV, is that we **can easily project ourselves.**

When I was a child, there was a TV show called 'Once upon a time…life', and in it, there was a **very visual explanation** of what was a sickness, virus and how our body can react. I just had to take these images for my visualisations. As my definition of subconscious in Hypnosis/Hypnosophy is **as a 5 year old child,** it was **a game I could easily jump into.**

I did have darker moments, and as I am very much a one emotion only kind of guy, it was **quite upsetting**. I didn't understand why, visualising these internal wars, the diminishing of this painful mass, it wouldn't reduce.

When we work as practitioners, it is frequent to see **exceptional things,** physical and psychological feedbacks that are quite impressive…so **there is some frustration** when personal feedbacks don't live up to our expectations. To note, **my tumor didn't grow more** with all the hours of work I put in each day. Unfortunately, it is a reflection I had, when I stopped these exercises and that it started to grow.

Chapter 10 : meeting my doctor

My body and I had **a deal**, I will 'handle it'until mid-July.

In one of my trances, I put in place an agreement between my body and my psyche. **My subconscious kept his word.** Was it a programmation or was it really the maximum I could hold out ? I can't tell, but, Thursday 12th July, symptoms of a **pain without name** started. I had the feeling that during the following 48 hours, I was living a pain from hell. As if my body was giving back for all I had made him go through since childhood. A fever over 39 degrees, deliriums, vomitting. And as my doctor was not able to give an emergency appointment, **I only was able to have an appointment on the following Monday...** I didn't have a single pill/medicine and I thought...that I will be able to handle it myself. Again, it is a **beautiful compulsion** from me, even if I couldn't, I handled it myself, alone. Result : two days of intense pain, where I had to crawl to go to the toilet, where my fever and deliriums were preventing me from calming my pains, as **trances were impossible**. It was by taking back my **yoga books** and testing a lot of postures (probably not well done anyway) that after two days...I finally found a posture to appease myself that allowed me to sleep.
When I had my appointment, it was already a few days I hadn't eaten anything...**I wasn't valiant.**

Now, I must say, my doctor is a bit particular. He is my doctor since I do not have a pediatrician. I never was really into 'doctors' so I only went when I needed aptitude certificates or was suffering from man flu. It was 3-4 years that I hadn't gone, I also should mention that he is a **hypnosis pratitioner, graduated** from a famous doctors'school. For the context, it was a Monday of the **second half of July (slowest time in France due to holidays),** let's say that I was coming at a bad time. During my appointment, I say that since January I have this ball and that it actually started a few months before… which **will cost me a severe reprimand.** Hey, when you go to the doctor, it is undubitably so that you can be told off like if you were five. It is very interesting to note that Medicine often puts us back into **a child status, adapted if possible,** that we find also in **Transactional Analysis**, as to engrave an **authority figure**, you would have first to build an **inferiority complex.** The only thing is that if we go back to the TA, I am a **rebellious child**, I hate being infantilised but mainly I think that for **a hypnotherapist,** he didn't understand anything about **indirect communication. He didn't even examine me,** he looked without getting close and told me it was probably an infection and that with antibiotics it will get better. Just to be sure, he proposed to me to do an echography. Two days later, I had my echography and looking at the **body langage of the specialist**, I didn't find him very comfortable.

When I asked him what did I have, he answered to me that maybe, I should go and see an **urologist.** That he couldn't say anything about it as it would be up to my doctor to speak with me. The only issue was that I talked to my doctor when I told him that the medicine was giving me new pains and that he asked me to stop them, and if my symptoms diminished…just before saying that he was **going on holidays the day after** and gave me a new appointment for beginning of August. Just at the end of the appointment…he made a fantastic suggestion... **"It is probably an infection ... maybe a cancer..."** For those who know a bit about hypnosis, you know that the **delay is a way to make a suggestion bigger…** what a great dexterity in conversational hypnosis was the one of my doctor.

Here we are, for the first time the **word 'Cancer'** has been said. In this part of the book, I am particularly going to **underline semantic**. I think that the medical staff do their best with their tools but **communication is essential.** We know that doctors are **authority figures,** moreover with the known experiences of **Milgram,** we know the **influence of the white coat syndrome.** Sickness is a **dissonant situation** for a patient, it is a moment that can be linked to an **emotional confusion.** And in its variations, **fear becomes one of the most important levers.** Fear of suffering, fear of death, fear of words, fear of consequences.

When a doctor talks, he/she becomes thus **one of the best hypnosis practitioners,** whithout knowing the ins and outs of the language. Doctors **influence** the perception of things, **orientate** the cognitive processes of their patient. We know that the **psychological aspects have a real impact** in the process of getting better. So…let's say that this appointment…**really made me angry**.

I thought it was unworthy of a doctor, especially a **hypnotherapist**. I took an appointment with an oncologist…who could only receive me the 28th of the following month. I had some tests, I saw again my doctor **for the last time** a few days before seing the urologist. He didn't give me more answers, and **I expected more.** The specialist on the other hand had **really been excellent.** A doctor who was on the verge of his retirement. Entering his practice, it went fast, clearly presented. He took a look, then with a tumor of 285 grams, quickly **agreed that it was a cancer.** He presented this without fioriture and was surprised I wasn't much more annoyed, he even smiled.

As it is **impossible to make a biopsy,** the only thing to do in this case, is to take out the tumor. **An ablation.** From there, I was able to see the medical machine starting.

Chapter 11 : The medical Machine starts

I was impressed by this world and **the very oiled mechanism of the medical body.**

A world which **'submits' us** to what the **'fair' doctors decide for us.** At this point, I am not sure that we are **'free'. Free** to live or die, to follow protocols or not, to listen… In reality, there is a **huge pressure.** As if not following automatically, meant we will endure a prejudice. I am not saying we shouldn't follow, my question is more, **can we really, in a fear and fragile state, decide** of anything…not counting the pressure of the medical staff, society and family ?

I have been called back a few hours later and **given** a date for the surgery and the details of the anaesthetist. It **all was starting,** and I needed to follow. All was planned so that the surgery happen two weeks later. However, I had a **competition** and as I like to make my own decisions, **I moved my surgery a week further...** Apparently it was not very well taken. I have been told that my **'situation' was urgent.** They were using **fear levers, guilt,** while explaining that they were going fast for my health.

My appointment with the anaesthetist was really instructive. He refused for me to have the **surgery under hypnosis** but was clearly interested in the method.

He explained to me that it might take time for clinics to generalise this technique.

To be **well prepared for the surgery**, I made some mp3 so that the surgery go well, for me to feel comfortable and so that I can recover fast. It is at this moment that I **diminished my daily discipline,** and that I saw the tumor growing a bit. I was surprised.

Chapter 12 : Surgery

I entered in the clinic a Sunday, the day after a competition, I was to stay until the following Thursday or Friday.

I thought that to **come the day before wasn't necessary**, a loss of time as there is no particular reason to do so…it can stress the partner…but I can also understand the administrative reasons. A funny detail, which will be later a little bit problematic, the clinic wasn't far from my place…so **I went there in motorcycle**. I didn't want to **annoy anyone**… I thought it would be easier. The day after, in the morning, the surgery was performed. I remember that my waking up has been violent, I was very agitated, I even punched a male nurse, saying that it was ok and that I could go back home now… I think **my subconscious didn't want to stay.**

In the evening, I negociated to **not have any pain killer.** Again, a little war with the medical staff who 'only follow indications'. I explained I was managing my pain but the nurse refused to listen. The day after, 6.30 am, the **doctor came and see me** to see if all was ok. I said yes and that I **was going to go back home.** He refused at first…but I wasn't in a mood to negociate. The detail I haven't thought of were my 13 stitches, I didn't test them. It is true that it took me **an hour to shower** and to put my clothes on before being able to get down and sign for my exit.

Then…This is when I laughed outloud…realising that it was going to be **impossible for me to ride my** motorcycle. I was to walk, to go back home. Christine proposed me to come and get me … but **as to be compulsive, let's go all the way with it** and… as a challenge towards my pain, **I walked back home**.

It was long, but really **satisfying for me.** Indeed, if I could, less than 24h after my surgery, walk…it was a **good sign**. Also, two days later I was to be able to give a **week end of courses** for learners.

Christine came in the morning to bring me some provisions, it was **really cool for her to do that**.

Now, I was awaiting the results to know which type of cancer it was.

Chapter 13 : Results

Thursday, with my team HnO, we are used to talk about hypnosis and then to go do some **urban hypnosis.**

After a whole day off, I went Place des Vosges (Paris) to talk and relax. I was able to ride my motorcycle, so I was able to go place to place.

You can't imagine the **satisfaction** I felt to this announce. It was funny to hear him say that the surgery was needed even if the cancer was necrosed. I asked how did the cancer got necrosed… **no answer.** After all, months of personal work seemed to have bear fruits… not in diminishing the tumor but in **necrosing it**. It was how **my subconscious saw the solution.**

No, though…it is not the end as I thought it would be. It is a new step and the medical world was about to put me again in their **infantilising machine**.

Chapter 14 : Ah, what needs to be followed ?

I think **I probably didn't listen really to what the doctor explained** to me about the process for cancer patient.

The following Monday I received a call from an oncologist practice, a colleague from my urologist, specialist in **followings**. The call was to **give me** a date for an appointment about the following. I was surprised as I **have never been in contact with them and that apparently I didn't need to for them to call me.** Therefore, **I refused.** I do not appreciate things imposed. I am not going to blame a compulsion…let's say that in transactional analysis, I was a **rebellious child.** Now, imagine the life of my parents…

A few days later, I called back to take myself an appointment. I let you imagine what the waiting room was like…It was **really instructive on a semantic point of view. Most people are weakened**, in chemo or in radiotherapy. They are accompanied and talk a lot. The **fear of death** is in all their words.

What impressed me the most, besides the fact that an oncologist is always an hour late, is the **absolute trust** that all of these people put in doctors. They repeat words said, **they wait for answers and solutions.** There is a real and **important form of dependance.** When I had my first consultation, I admit that I **had no idea what it was for.**

The oncologist was cold, a professional, nothing to add. He knows his work. After a few exchanges, he talk to me about **chemotherapy.** I think I probably had a **beautiful negative hallucination.** And to not hear this word…a **denial.** So, he explains to me that, **preventive chemo** is really important to avoid sick cells to generate another cancer. Even if **the tumor was necrosed,** there is no guarantee that other cells are not sick aswell. I can't remember if it is at this consultation or the following one that I refused the chemo.

Something really made me angry, as you can see I **still have a work on anger to do**. I work on it, but it takes longer than a cancer to deal with. The doctor, when I refused, presented me **statistics and the dangers to not follow with chemotherapy.** Recidivism, problems that can occur, the possibility to die. I found this…**great.** I thought that with these statistics, with this mathematical truth of death sentence, people probably change their mind quite quickly. If we go back to the hypnotic communication, the **authority link with the death lever,** is very powerful. And the medical machine doesn't propose anything, but **impose…** surgery, appointment, protocols…it is hard to **'be responsible for your own life'.** On the other hand, if a patient (me in this case) decides to not follow protocols, then, we can feel that **the grain of sand is not welcome in the machine.** Again, if you are sick…follow medical directives.

At first, my oncologist didn't know what to say, and most of all, **din't know what process to put in place.** With a lot of honesty and that is, I think, something I really appreciate in some of them. He had to look into european protocols, and after studying the question, he talked to me about **scouring** (I do not know what it is but I am not a fan or surgery and follow ups). To be clear, he never has done any following and **didn't know at all how to do it.** It is an interesting proof, which indicate that patients refuse only very rarely **what the machine propose.** Which is good to cured an illness.

But before anything, he tried to **seed doubts**, saying that I will most likely be sick again under a two years time, and that I will still need to do a PET scan. I accept and did all the complementary exams, to be able to finally **start my following.** For passionate of NLP and indirect hypnosis, there is an interesting thing I put in place with my doctor. I must admit, I am **an annoying patient**, and I can imagine that my energy during my appointments were not presenting me very opened. Then, as I told myself I didn't have to be unpleasant with a man who was doing well his job, I **changed my way of being**. I took back the **NLP principles,** on relation and in order to observe all **micro expressions**. It has been significative, during the session, for a feedback of one of my scans. He started to laugh and I made him talk about his work, on how did he become oncologist.

I learnt a lot, in particular that he was doing consultations because, on the opposite of his colleagues, he **loved human contact,** and that he was considering humans. It has been a revealer. The way many doctors do clumsy things really do come from a **lack of knowledge** on this part.

The factor of communication is now a factor of **techniques.** They want to share a message, and to do so, use the emotional and its management, but they are **complex to handle.**

Chapter 15 : Cancer and others

This a very important chapter for me.

I didn't talk about my cancer. I think that outside of my compulsion **to not be weak,** I believe that people we love **shouldn't be affected by our issues.** My family didn't know and within my group of friends, except Christine, **nobody knew.** I realised that the word 'cancer' was settling people into a **fear state and discomfort.** Let's be honest, I love to do it during conversations. To see reactions, corporal withdrawals and **powerless sensation.** It is because of this powerless sensation that I think **it is not necessary to talk about** it. **What could your loved ones do when you** are sick ? **I am the one living the sickness and noone can know** or feel what is happening in my body or head. I have been told that the presence and the love of your loved ones are important to handle your sickness. How do an external person **'measure' his/her presence and love acts ?** I know that if I had talk to my parents, I would have witness my mother moving in **with all of her love, packed in baggages,** and my father too.

As I wrote, I was spending **normal days,** I was working on me, on my partners, was training. Many people who love their closest ones do not realise, that they can become **suffocating.** I think that the one we love, we want them happy, we want them to evolve easily into their lives.

With my parents, I think (and probably I am wrong) that they already have done their job and that they don't have **to stress and forget themselves** for their son. It is a projection, I know it, but to be an adult, for me, is about handling my issues alone. Sickness builds **anxiety,** that the patient needs to handle, but **the loved ones live it too**. They speculate, and try to do good but in my opinion **they will then be hurt**. If I had talk about my sickness, I could have make sick the one I care the most about. It is a **trauma chock** principle which works like **patterns rupture** and offers to subconscious a way to express sometimes by **generating an illness**. So I didn't say a word. Some people asked me **if it has been hard to not say**. They were projecting that I was suffering, but really, **I was happy of my experience**, happy to be able to see, **without any moral or social limits**, if what I am passionated about, what which take all seconds of my life since years, **will work**.

A **great experience of life.** Certainly more calm than other cancers. Can you imagine that your friend, your son, tells you : **'Don't worry, I can handle it.** I have psycho energetic techniques to test on me.'
Do you think you would let him do it ? If you love the person, would you have accept to let this person test on himself ?

Chapter 16 : And since then

Today, **it has been two years that the surgery has been done,** I am still followed and apparently everything is fine.

On the other hand, my body and my hormones went to plan B. Yes, I often say to my partners and learners that we are extraordinary, that we can easily to move on to other steps. I am convinced that when **we have open the spiritual Pandora's box,** we are just going to carry on for the rest of our lives. It is the metaphor of the **onion layer**. When we enter into the world of the **internal search**, we enter a long path which can be interminable. When we take out a layer…there is another one under. Sometimes, we stop taking out layers, **we are tired of crying**. Sometimes we carry one.

For me, even if I am a bit tired to always try to go deeper, **I know that I am not yet enough listening**, and that **I am still not in the true and fair**. And my body reminds me of this, certainly because my subconscious saturated from repeating it…and that I never stop to find new techniques, instead of just **accepting it as it is.** Outside of the fact that **hormones get excited a bit**, my body, him, decided to **take on weight.** It is not only linked to hormones, weight is an **excellent protector** when it is said to the subconscious that in the next 2 to 5 years…we could die.

Moreover, 2 months later, I made the mistake to fight a guy who was 70 kg more than myself and who **damaged my cervicals.** As I do a lot of fights without limits of weight, my subconscious told me : 'Here we go, **let's bring something else again...**' I work everyday on **different problematics** which, in my opinion, are not necessarly easier than the one I had during my cancer. Sometimes, I think that it is **even more delicate without remarkable symptoms.** My everyday work is **still intense,** as I was saying to friends who know about the Enneagram, the more I work on me, the more I am compulsive.

I ask myself sometimes if **working on yourself really bring only good.** It is engaging, but we can discover many shadows of this obscurity **which can devour us.** On this way, there are many **beautiful waves of light** and it is agreeable to **lose yourself in it,** never really knowing if you are in an illusion of appeasement or if you are on an evolutionary path.

Conclusion

As expressed in other essays, **therapy is a quest.** It is like the path taken by the Alchemist or the Little Prince. We are in a **search.** One of a balance, fairness and truth. I walk that path and sometimes, some heavier things **come in the way**. Just to make me take the time to understand better who we are and **what we can do.**

Here are some reflections on a practitioner who observe with amusement experiences that he imposes on himself. In this **desire to 'know', to find more 'real' and 'true'.** I am not saying that I won't have other sicknesses, or that what I have done once would work again. What I can say is that **discipline and hypnotic methods** can bring positive feedbacks. In my case, a necrosed tumor. It allows to calm down pain, temperature and discomfort. **Auto-analysis and auto-hypnosis works** bring understanding, a way to let go of many neuroses.

Hypnosis is a discipline.

Who is Christophe Pank ?

I am French and live in Paris. I have worked in hypnosis, NPL, personal development and energetic healing for more than a decade. Everyday, I share my experience and knowledge. To optimise my work, I created HnO (Hype-N-Ose) Hypnose in 2010. As psycho-practitioner, I can help people to learn about themselves, to increase their knowledge.

I am now sharing my ideas in essays, videos and audios. The more you open your mind to different ways of thinking, the more you develop your capacity to become who you really are.

Take the time to watch my english Youtube Channel : hnohypnosis and my website : www.hnohypnosis.com